King Nebuchadnezzar had a very long name that was hard to spell.
He was also the rich king of Babylon, thousands of years ago. Babylon
was the biggest empire in the world, but the king wanted more.
So he captured the city of Jerusalem.

A young man named Daniel, was one of the captured people who was taken to Babylon. Daniel loved God and wanted to please Him.

The king put the smartest young men from Jerusalem into a special school. Daniel was also chosen, and he learned the ways of the Babylonians.

The king gave the students his best food. But that was a problem for Daniel, because Daniel followed God's rules and only ate healthy foods.

The people of Babylon didn't know the true God, and so they ate whatever they wanted. Like huge greasy pizzas, triple topping ice-cream and cake galore ... at every meal.

It looked yummy. But Daniel knew it wasn't going to feel yummy in his tummy. Besides, it was against God's menu, and God knows best.

Daniel and his friends where finally allowed to eat the healthy foods they requested. After 10 days, thy were healthier and stronger than all the other students.

God blessed Daniel with wisdom, and he became a very smart man to help the king.

One night, king Nebuchadnezzar had a strange dream. It woke him up in a fright. "What does this dream mean?" he wondered.

So the King called all the smart guys together, to tell him the dream and what it means. "That's impossible. We can't do that!" they said. And they were right, because only God can answer that.

The king was angry, and wanted to get rid of them all. But Daniel asked for some time to pray to God about it. The king calmed down and agreed.

Sometime later, Daniel came to the king. "This is your dream, and what it means..." he began. "God has shown it to me."

The king listened carefully and realized that it was a message from God. The king rewarded Daniel and put him in charge of important things of Babylon.

Some of the kings helpers didn't like Daniel. Now Daniel was more important than they were. They where jealous and planned to get him into trouble.

With a sneaky plan, they got the king to make a new rule: "No one is allowed to pray to their God for 30 days. Those who disobey will be fed to the lions."

Daniel read the law, but the next morning he went to his room and prayed to God anyway. The same as he did every morning, noon and night.

"We finally caught him disobeying the king. Now we can get him into big trouble." said the jealous helpers. And they ran to tell the king.

The king was sad that he had been tricked into making the silly law.
But even he could not change it now. So Daniel was arrested.

"May your God save you!" the king called to Daniel, as Daniel was carried to the lions as their snack.

The king could not eat. He could not sleep either. All he could do was think of his friend, Daniel.

Daniel did not sleep either. He prayed for God to protect him.

God heard Daniel's prayers again, and sent an Angel to keep the lions from munching on Daniel. They did not even touch him.

The next morning, the king rushed to see what had become of Daniel. Daniel was found alive and well. "Get him out at once!" the king said to the guards. "And throw these bad men in instead."

The king made a new law: "People everywhere should honor and respect the true God that Daniel serves!"

iCHARACTER

Published by iCharacter Ltd. (Ireland)
www.icharacter.org
By Agnes and Salem de Bezenac
Illustrated by Agnes de Bezenac
Copyright 2015. All rights reserved.

Copyright © 2015 by iCharacter Ltd.. All rights reserved. No part of this book may be reproduced in any form or by any electronic or mechanical means, including information storage and retrieval systems, without written permission from the publisher or author, except in the case of a reviewer, who may quote brief passages embodied in critical articles or in a review.

www.ingramcontent.com/pod-product-compliance
Lightning Source LLC
Chambersburg PA
CBHW081503070526
44586CB00019B/2465